P9-AEW-595

PRAISE FOR HAFIZAH GETER'S *UN-AMERICAN*

"In *Un-American*, Hafizah Geter creates a new kind of portraiture. A family is slowly etched in relief in language both lush and exacting. This gorgeous debut troubles and reshapes notions of belonging against the backdrop of a country obsessed with its own exclusions, erasures, borders, institutions, and violence. Geter's poems simmer original forms of witness and resistance." *—Claudia Rankine*, author of *Citizen*

"Hafizah Geter's *Un-American* reads like a high lyric conversation overheard. Poem after poem, the most ordinary of items—cups, cards, couches—get ratcheted up into their proper glory. In other words, Geter sees the world as a stage set for what she needs to tell her family but can't, what she needs to hear from her family but won't. And all of this is done with attention to what this one beautiful story says about the so-called American story." *—Jericho Brown*, author of *The Tradition*

"Hafizah Geter's heart-rending poetry embodies the union between experiences. This timely and powerful book speaks to the struggles of two nations, and to the grace of the invincible light of black life." *—Rigoberto González*, author of *The Book of Ruin*

"Unflinching and undeniable, Hafizah Geter's *Un-American* shows how trust and faith fail across continents, as legacies of brutal loss written in blood and memory inhabit the haunted present—'together, slowly domesticating / our suffering.' The poems hold a narrative clarity that edges against exile's reverberating consequences, and in gorgeous language deliver a trenchant understanding of which worlds one can and cannot inhabit, ever aware of both the power of imagination—and its limits. The testimonies of the dead and the living haunt this book. Are we paying attention yet?" *—Khadijah Queen*, author of *Anodyne*

"Here is the history of this country in all its blood and complication, with all its promise and betrayal. These poems are an accounting, a testimony, a prayer—poems meant to quiet the animal inside us. A beautiful book." *—Nick Flynn*, author of *I Will Destroy You*

"Hafizah Geter's collection, *Un-American*, is the book I wish I had in my youth as I tried to negotiate the difficult terrain of identity, citizenship, self and nation. Luckily, I embrace this collection now at the beginning of a new decade . . . a book filled with hymns, anthems, testimonies in remembrance of

Sandra Bland, Michael Brown, and Tamir Rice. It is also a book of waking dreams that travels through Nigeria, South Carolina, Alabama, Chicago, and Beijing as it seeks to find shelter for the restless body as seen through the eyes of a daughter as she is witness to the tender allegiance and wounds of family. This is a collection we should all be reading. All that needs to be said is said in the fertile land of this book. Hafizah Geter sings a complicated song of God, country, and the search for belonging. Each revelation is unbearable. Each revelation is something we should all bear." —**Tina Chang**, author of *Hybrida*

"In this remarkable debut, Hafizah Geter troubles the meaning of 'protection,' an abstraction made painfully real in poems that examine family love, family secrets, home, language, and faith. Geter takes us inside one particular family where 'fireworks splash against my parents' / American Dream,' a family composed of a Muslim mother from Nigeria, a U.S.-born black artist father, and two foreign-born daughters raised in the U.S. The lens keeps mostly a tight focus as we come to know, and feel for, the imperfect but beloved mother and father, a legacy of abuse, and the unresolved tension between a desire to assimilate and the need to retain one's own identity and tongue. The speaker's name translates as 'Protector,' and we see her in the impossible role of protecting her mother and father, her sister, her nephew; the desire to protect, and the failure to protect show up in the four poems titled 'Testimony,' which speak to, from, and against racial violence. The collection feels like a novel that captures intimate details and portrays a larger landscape of racial and cultural discrimination and danger. Time boomerangs us into new places, confronts us with absences that turn back into presences that turn back into irrevocable losses. And irony courses through these searingly beautiful poems, an irony fueled by and perhaps even tamed by a profound empathetic love that makes the truths revealed here that much more painful. Yes, this is a speaker who can say 'My grass-stained knees pledge allegiance / to a country that belongs to no one / I love.' And we understand that belonging is the problem here, not love. The speaker, 'a two-citizen child' with 'no country,' is both helpless witness and brilliant anatomist of a nation's hypocrisies and violences. 'How to Bring Your Children to America' is a stunning poem at the center of this urgent collection that reads like a whirlwinded, torn-up, and collaged coming-of-age story deeply complicated by race, faith, contemporary politics and violence. Geter's vertiginous figuration—a mother is 'my rope / through the sea'; a father 'swallows / the landscape in his hands'; the daughters are 'new / dictionaries'; the speaker's 'longing could drive a car'—is an act of transformation that ferries love into poems of unapologetic and enlarging testimony." —**Catherine Barnett**, author of *Human Hours*

UN-AMERICAN

HAFIZAH GETER

WESLEYAN

POETRY

*

WESLEYAN

UNIVERSITY

PRESS

*

MIDDLETOWN,

CONNECTICUT

CARLSBAD CITY LIBRARY
CARLSBAD CA 92011
DISCARD

UN-AMERICAN

CO
811.6
GET

Wesleyan University Press

Middletown CT 06459

www.wesleyan.edu/wespress

2020 © Hafizah Augustus Geter

All rights reserved

Manufactured in the United States of America

Designed by Crisis and typeset in Freight and Halyard

Cover painting: Tyrone Geter, *Nine Months*

Lines from "Farewell," from *The Country
Without a Post Office* by Agha Shahid Ali,
copyright © 1997 by Agha Shahid Ali, used by
permission of W. W. Norton & Company, Inc.

Library of Congress Cataloging-in-Publication

Names: Geter, Hafizah, 1984– author.

Title: Un-american / Hafizah Geter.

Description: Middletown, Connecticut : Wesleyan University Press, [2020] |
Series: Wesleyan poetry | Summary: "Poetry that investigates definitions of
belonging in relation to migration, religion, language, and loss, tracing a family
history between Nigeria and the United States"— Provided by publisher.

Identifiers: LCCN 2020022331 | ISBN 9780819579805 (cloth) |
ISBN 9780819579812 (trade paperback) | ISBN 9780819579829 (ebook)

Subjects: LCSH: Belonging (Social psychology)—Poetry. | LCGFT: Poetry.

Classification: LCC PS3607.E885 U53 2020 | DDC 811/.6—dc23

LC record available at https://lccn.loc.gov/2020022331

5 4 3 2 1

DEC - 1 2020

FOR MY PARENTS

HAUWA TINI ADAMU GETER & **TYRONE GETER,**

& MY SISTER **JAMILA TANI**

& FOR MY GRANDMOTHERS

GUSSIE MAE SIMON & **HANNATU SALEH ADAMU**

I am everything you lost. You won't forgive me.

My memory keeps getting in the way of your history.

AGHA SHAHID ALI

CONTENTS

II.

.

III.

THE PLEDGE

With dirt under her fingernails our mother held our father's hands

the years marked hoping one of his paintings would sell

the two of them always in search of

auspices their daughters, their last blood

my sister and I we were jackknives

a long division splitting them continents wide

Seeds blown and planted Zaria to Boston

black fruit of Akron winters Africans hyphenated down to a promise

cultivated inside the sunlit chains of our father's South

while our mother resurrected in the dark her prayers

our half-grief the spell of protection

She told us what *He* would not give us

we were forbidden to name, but *Allah* like color staining a porcelain sink

I've lain with women our mother lost to myth

I am a test of how far a daughter's memory can go

Our father, a wilted shoot of wheat wavering against the wind, never expected to age

alone in his birth country Our bondage stretches

our ghosts in all directions trying to out-pick the rot

America has grown in our throats

THE LIFE OF A CELL

In my parents' first house

termites gathered,

the floorboards opening to a circle

of jaws, that certain

proximity required for one kind of creature

to make illness in another.

Inside my mother, my father fell

into a deep sleep.

A decade of wet wood

pressed its mouth to theirs.

It takes a million gods

to create a single mercy.

My mother opened

her legs, prayed to only Allah.

Shared, rented,

occupied, my mother breathed

so hard it rained

through the roof.

I scurried from her,

a splinter

between my teeth.

NAMING CEREMONY

My father, who spends most of his days painting

pictures, says coming home to my mother

stroking out was like walking in on an affair.

Bending, he demonstrates how

an aneurysm hugged her

to her knees. Over and over,

my father draws a loss

so big it is itself an inception, a story

he knows better than the day

his daughters were born.

Every retelling different:

bluer, then redder.

His memory bruising the neck

of whomever he can will

to listen.

His heart is strong.

He has the receipts:

a scar on his breast

that I've cleaned like a smudge on a window.

Over and over, my father draws me

a picture of the crescent moon

fishhooking her hospital room.

He loses the story

for the pleasure of finding it,

his tongue the builder

of a maze. I can tell you

our best days weren't glad.

He's a history

whittled down to this

single story. In my version,

when her mind blew,

boys I barely knew

played Beirut, cans of Pabst

crushed against their shoulders,

white balls flicking

into crimson solo cups,

the night lost to the drawl

of a far-gone gurney.

F A J R

Disease my mother buried

like a baby. Days slept away,

blinds drawn. My father's forgotten Baptist prayers

from behind their bedroom wall

while my sister and I drew dreamcatchers, strings

turned hangman. In the Ohio dark,

coyotes nuzzled the neck of a swan.

The sun and the sky and the blood.

Days later, my mother

jail-sprung. Morning

returning her Fajr. My sister and I,

light in our Catholic school uniforms,

sneaking out to poke the swan's

pregnant body, curious

the shape death would take and wanting

to prove small women could be

kings. Behind us, my mother shuffling

in the houselight, a body rearranging

its omens. Quiet in both directions,

save the blood.

It was the year

the almonds didn't shell right

and waiting was its own tenderness.

All our ghosts have come

down from their mountain.

We have so many gods

and none of them

can be trusted.

THE BREAK IN

When I close my eyes, I see my mother running
from one house to another, throwing her fist
at neighbors' front doors, begging anyone to call
the police. There are times when every spectator is
hungry, times a thief takes nothing, leaves you a fool
in your inventory.
How one trespass could make all others
suddenly visible. My mother counted
her jewelry and called
overseas. My father counted women
afraid one of us would go
missing. When I close my eyes
I hear my mother saying, *A'aha, this new country,*
my cousins exclaiming, *Auntie!,*
between the clicking line and their tongues.
Tonight the distance between me, my mother, and Nigeria
is like a jaw splashed against a wall.
I close my eyes and see my father
sulking like a pile of ashes,
his hair jet black and kinky,
his silence entering a thousand rooms.
Then outside, trimming hedges as if home
were a land just beyond the lawn,

the leaves suddenly black.
When I close my eyes,
I see my mother, mean for the rest of the day,
rawing my back in the tub
like she's still doing dishes.

SALAH

Before Fajr, my sister digs
her toes in the lake

where blue-throated robins
have continued to gather.

Today is one place to bury a child
and what you say after.

Or else today is just domestic work.
How her bare knee touched mine,

the fern finding its way
back to life.

Today is not a crown,
it is the forceps, the sunken

flower of my sister's waist.
Today it only took a minute

to discover who among us was cruel.
We know better than to have

daughters now.
Today is the scar I put on

her thigh, how we've become heirs
to each other's hunger.

Kiss her
and the throne sits empty.

Today my sister is a door
put on backwards.

But maybe snow
finds the cypress—

Or, at best, the blue
robins return.

Or maybe today is just another day
between the small

humiliations.
So many times

I have pulled my sister's bones apart.
Took the femur

from the tibia. I buried my sister
in the backyard; can't tell you

how long I have knelt
to this regret.

Today my sister's teeth are slats
on the broken bridge between us.

We bare our elbows
one sleeve at a time

while doing dishes,
the bedsheets hung to dry,

her husband's stain
growing darker and darker.

NATURALIZED CITIZEN

Mouthing amendments, our mother studied

the Constitution. Her whisper

not English, not her

Hausa tongue,

but something lower—

a car revving its engine.

Our mother memorized presidents, capital cities,

adopted habits like moving

her green card from one closet to another,

kept a manila folder for every year of her life.

In the kitchen she turned Cream

of Wheat into tuwo shinkafa,

cooked kuka until our Catholic school jumpers stunk

of crushed baobab leaves. She'd spend days in

her garden refusing to explain anything

but the marigolds.

In America, no one would say her name

correctly. I watched it rust

beneath the salt of so many tongues

like a pile of crushed Chevys.

At night, she prayed to Allah

for something from America that was more

than children. Come weekends,

we were counting

the naira in her underwear drawer.

From her calling cards, we learned

Naa goodee meant

thank you.

Kai!,

everything else.

HYMN

At nine,

my father can't stop

placing a shotgun near the temple

of my great-grandfather,

who can't stop

pulling switches from Alabama

river birch,

nor unbuckling the unbloomed

hips of my aunts,

who now cover their couches

in plastic, their lips damp

in a fever hum of *Amens*,

potpourri coating them like wool.

By eleven, my father knows

the way moonshine rattles

inside a grown man,

cannot remove the rot

that roots my aunts

beneath the trunk of my great-grandfather,

their Sunday dresses crumpled

like roses, smiles hard

as Baptist pews.

VISITING PROPHETS

1

My uncle pacing the dirt field behind his mother's house,
like a car whose tank will not empty.
He might as well be in prison.

Poisoned

We guess,

bipolar

2

that maybe the malaria
is at it again.

If this were America, he would be a boat we could tug
beneath the shed during winters

or at the very least we could fix this fucking
limp.

If this were anywhere, we would be hysterical.
So long it's been since relief has doubled

us over, cried into our stomachs,
held our knees to our shoulders.

3

But since this is our homeland, we drive.

Through markets.
Past Ahmadu Bello University,
where my father taught students to draw the body
after mastering the line.

4

Into the brunt of a fresh
rainy season, my cousin snakes
the car round the roundabout,
round the beggars using foreign objects
as limbs. We are stockpiling

mangos, plantains, a bit
more powdered milk,
and baobab leaves for kuka.

Guards barely old enough to be lovers
stand in front of gated compounds
avoiding eyes and forgetting
the weight of their weapons, forgetting
our mothers have died
the same way.

5

What do we name this revision
of our bodies?

~~Diabetes~~
~~Hypertension~~
~~Hepatitis~~
~~Stroke~~

I can see how all these guns have helped
keep my uncle crazy.

Our hunger is anonymous.

6

For three days my feet continue
to swell, splitting

the stitching of the boots that took my last
eighty dollars. Not even

Nikes can hold me.
Maybe my uncle

is onto something,
pacing the backyard
of his mind.

7

On our mothers' dirt
roads we know

how dangerous someone
who wants to save you
can become.

Compassion is not the same as repair.

8

Let's say madness has a heart.

UN-AMERICAN

My mother transfers the last marigold

from a pot to a patch of earth

that she's carefully bellied out

beneath her, the dirt cool as a penny,

her fingers tender with the bright

petals as she demonstrates how

what's uprooted can return

to solid ground,

her colonial English helpless

against her native tongue's prayers.

Allāhu Akbar, my mother says as casually

as she says my name.

The wind, warmer

than the water from her morning wudu,

continues its pilgrimage East,

a steady stream

of fireworks chasing it in the distance.

My mother looks at me all shine,

her dreams quietly

wild in her garden.

She says the rain can do

in Nigeria what no sun will ever

do here in South Carolina,

her shadow my only relief

from the Confederate heat.

High noon, work done,

my mother settles in on the front porch

where my father swallows

the landscape in his hands.

Leaning over his shoulder,

she watches him sketch

another promise—

his wife and last child digging

in the garden. Our likenesses,

figurines, forever

in a charcoal

amber. In his mind,

my father is always building

shelter, the spirits that haunt him

like mice in the walls:

oranges for Christmas,

a single pair of khakis

to last all year, his mother

on her knees

Murphy oiling a white woman's Alabama

home. The heat licks the corners

of my father's sketchbook to a curl.

He draws God's shadow right

down to the horns.

In the garden, the bees burn

their tongues on sprouting

chili peppers, turning the honey mad.

Fireworks splash against my parents'

American Dream, a switch that turns

all their ghosts on.

Children prowl the streets

with sparklers in hand

impatient for the holiday to dusk.

I look for the ones like me and my sister

who, not born in this country,

can never be president.

My sister, upstairs, asleep

in the relief of this Independence.

Returned from college,

she's still never shed the gait

of our barely remembered home country.

My longing could drive a car—

citizen I am

to our parents' wounds.

My sister's and my blood the scar

healed between them. Half of us

never owned. Half,

Southern-lynched. Strange fruit.

Watch as I pull the slave out

of me. How un-American,

to wear the names

of what they fled.

My grass-stained knees pledge allegiance

to a country that belongs to no one

I love.

The mothers became targets.

Hanging on clotheslines, bibs

of the barely fed.

Children, countries born

split in two—firstborns

whose first steps aborted

their sisters, brothers, the fresh bread

of their love language,

children the English

tearing sphincters in two.

The mothers came by boat,

with wings, forgetting

their own mothers' uteruses, singing

praises to Allah, they came over and over again

until it could not matter that so-and-so had died,

we were the nicknames escaping

their bellies, the translation between

stay and *never arrived.*

Husbands, uncles, we were

wives, illnesses, pawpaw seeds,

only things that could save them,

sickle cells that knew better

than to touch. Visible

only in their dialect, they sent for cousins,

wired money, forgave ancestors

we couldn't trust.

They stopped speaking to us

in our birth language until we became new

dictionaries, became the consonants

of the Constitution they studied,

our first words forgotten

artifacts in our home

countries. They were the ones

whose fathers had died

in the milt of language,

without daughters.

In America, we were memories

without accents or consensus,

lambs that couldn't be traded

for milk, meal, or honey,

the fact of our bodies

in America their new Quran.

And, oh, how they moaned,

how they starved, sucking their teeth

between King's English, yelling for us

to stop playing immigrant and go

get naturalized.

TESTIMONY

FOR SANDRA BLAND, 1987–2015

After the miscarriage, she moved to Waller County

wearing the ghost of motherhood

and wanting to make old wounds foreign.

In my bedroom, I read aloud the list

of her contusions, watched an officer

drag her from her car over and over again.

As if the humiliations would never be done,

there were typos in her autopsy report.

The words: no signs of struggle.

I thought: her body is my body, is a church

set fire, is the toil that makes the land,

a jail cell, light as a paper bag,

the sound my father makes

when, after so many years, he says my mother's name.

Twenty-eight,

they split her open where slaves grew

cotton at the banks of the Brazos and students

at Prairie View A&M can barely vote

and laid her bare—a coroner's wishbone

carved in her chest.

In Waller County, they still segregate

their cemeteries, name

some murders suicide.

They fire their police chief,

vote him Sheriff.

ALABAMA PARABLE

My father leans down the barrel of a shotgun house

and looks in both directions.

At one end, my great-grandfather is leaking

like smoke from my aunt's room,

where, in her body, he has left

the smell of fire. At the other end,

my grandmother, Gussie Mae:

a bull reluctantly

bound to her matador.

It is barely a secret

that this man is the one thing

all the women in my family have in common.

My father calls it a night

so dark the dark

could have been broken,

teaches me the hardest thing is to be loved

by a woman you can't protect.

My father looks down the barrel

of a shotgun house,

sees in my grandmother

hurt like prayer

is a kneeling position,

sees that fearing

the wrath of God can make you

name any angry man, King.

He still hesitates during a storm

because once upon a time

thunder meant the Lord

was working,

warns his girls

to recognize the certain mole

that marks men willing

to pay for moonshine

but never rent, says to go

for the knees, throat, eyes.

He moves like his whole

life depends on superstition,

sleeps like he's listening—

for the creaking door, the smoke signals,

the witnesses—to my aunts' fires.

Seventy-two and tired of keeping secrets,

every Christmas my father gifts me another,

each an heirloom wrapped

tightly in his mouth.

Lesson one: there's no god

in Alabama. Lesson two:

where the road forks

between faith

and survival. Lesson three:

Know my grandmother

did the best she could.

The kill shot: to leave

a wounded thing

with its heart still beating.

TESTIMONY

FOR ERIC GARNER, 1970–2014

Daylight,
and they dug

their fingers
into my rectum.

Was it intimacy? Was it
search? Was it

seizure? Bystander
footage,

marker 4:33,
I become

a broken bridge.
A wound

beneath the belly
of a city wolf. Judge,

they censor the air
and I see my children's faces.

This love is blue-
collar work, this exile,

heritage. I don't regret
the kings and queens I've made,

though police keep fucking
up. Keep kicking

down the door
inside me. Master's tools steady

trying to burn our cribs down.
My children search mirrors

for suspicious activity. Marker 4:40.
The hourglass imitates

me. Judge, the wolves,
they multiply.

So intimate, come marker 5:03,
their skin takes

custody, my breath
away.

EID AL-ADHA

Maybe, I love the pain in her best.
How long she can make one meal last.

Having oversalted the cod,
our mother rinses

its mouth in the sink,
brushing from head to tail.

It's her first time out of bed
since Sunday. All the lights inside her flicker.

Our gods loosen
their chains. She believes

the wind can split
a single seed. That she can drive her body

into resurrecting. Between her shoulders,
medicine accumulates.

The sun performs its evening
Maghrib. She washes away

each coarse grain, finally free
from the memory of the monger.

MY BROTHER-IN-LAW RECITES THE TAKBIR

In the revolving door of my sister's apartment,
my brother-in-law kneels East, palms the Quran,

searching for Mecca. Feet washed,
he crosses arms over chest

drowning the days as heavy stones
in supplication. My sister,

confusing devotion
with taking him back, bows

by his side. It is a sight
that makes my knees buckle

so beautiful and familiar
to the days I spent prostrate,

mimicking the raka'āt of our mother's
morning prayers,

the beads of her misbaha
squeezed tightly between

my fingers
as I sung the ninety-nine names

of Allah. The first time
my brother-in-law leaves,

his shadow in the bedsheets
is the braille

my sister deciphers her swollen belly
across. The second time, she comes

to sleep at my house,
their new son

at her nipple like a hooked fish.
It is winter in Chicago.

My brother-in-law,
having shattered

every syllable between them, turns
silence into metaphor.

My sister prays towards the god
of our mother and our memories.

A god I hope would rather
throw away a miracle

than bend an ear
towards the wishes

of a father who has weaponized
leaving. My sister

looks out into her life
cooled by the breeze

of a door slamming. A man
who only looks back

when returning.
My brother-in-law is home

again. I cradle their son in my arms
so they can pray.

Enough history between us
that my nephew calms quickly, reaches

towards my chest
as if searching

for my sister's residue, his eyes
so new they are my prayer.

With my nephew in my arms
the only thing between Allah and me

are two cans and a string.
My brother-in-law's need

a valley, my sister's a mirror.
With his eyes wide

open, my brother-in-law raises both hands
and recites the Takbir, the storm in him

quelling to a melody and already I know
the next time he leaves

my sister will invite him back
into her body,

her temperature just beginning
to drop

after carrying the weight
of two heartbeats.

TESTIMONY

FOR TAMIR RICE, 2002–2014

Mr. President,

After they shot me they tackled my sister.

The sound of her knees hitting the sidewalk

made my stomach ache. It was a bad pain.

Like when you love someone

and they lie to you. Or that time Mikaela cried

all through science class and wouldn't tell anyone why.

This isn't even my first letter to you,

in the first one I told you about my room

and my favorite basketball team

and asked you to come visit me in Cleveland

or send your autograph. In the second one

I thanked you for your responsible citizenship.

I hope you are proud of me too.

Mom said you made being black beautiful again

but that was before someone killed Trayvon.

After that came a sadness so big it made *everyone*

look the same. It was a long time before we could

go outside again. Mr. President it took one whole day

for me to die and even though I'm twelve and not afraid of the dark

I didn't know there could be so much of it

or so many other boys here.

TESTIMONY

FOR MICHAEL BROWN, 1996–2014

For hours I lay there,
sun at my back,
my blood running a country

mile between the pavement
and the crown of my head.
Officer, no ambulance ever came.

It took a long time to cover my body.
There are politics to death
and here politics performs

its own autopsies. My aunties
say things like, *Boy big, black as you.*
Then, the prosecution rests.

My neighbors never do. They lose
sleep as the National Guard parades
down Canfield. I heard my blood

was barely dry. I heard there were soldiers
beating their shields like war cries,
my boys holding hands

through the tear gas. Heard my mother

wandered the streets,

her body trembling

between a prayer

and a fist. I heard a rumor

about riots got started.

Officer, I heard that after so much blood,

the ground develops

a taste for it.

THE LEAVING

A Nigerian proverb

that when you lose your bridge,

climb down the mountain.

Instead, my mother grabbed

the Atlantic. Enough for a path

to carry daughters.

Every mile of seabed leapt over

used to form statues

of her brothers

in her mind. On her back,

I slept a journey.

She whispered, *leave*

our language behind, afraid

of an old country

on my tongue.

In America,

feet never dried.

Half-breed turned hemlock.

My mother, my rope

through the sea, my vine.

I arrived, language's orphan,

a two-citizen child, no country.

Wake, a dead woman's

daughter, homesick with no home

to ill towards, listening

for what English does

to my blood.

FAMILY PORTRAIT

Upstream,
the salmon fail,

winter catches them
one freezing current at a time—

we lose
the oak first,

roots crown, tired
with the earth

as we are with the animal
inside us that we have failed

to quiet. Winter
is an old milk

we leave
for the missing,

a starving flame
that calls

the unnamed
fox.

OUT OF AFRICA

After so long, our father wants to go home
to the continent that named my mother.
As soon as next July, my sister says
over Skype while, outside my window,
New York rain fails to snuff summer's fires.

The older she gets, the more I see
how her six years in Nigeria rival my three,
how the memory of the land wisps from the switch
of her wrists, how African she must seem,
a Muslim raising two black boys in Beijing,

locals crouching to take my nephews'
photos on daily outings. Her youngest, three, screaming, *no!*,
his skin so black it is bright. On the screen,
the oldest, eight, fills his mouth
with all the Mandarin and Arabic

his smile can muster. Proudly, he shows me all he has of his stepfather's
Jola and Wolof. Something in my sister knows
it is easier in China than America to give her children
uncolonized language, easier to raise black boys to be men
who never forget duty or home.

Months and months before her stroke,

our mother began looking like a woman

who would never see hers again. She read

Candide, gave cousins uncharacteristically tearful goodbyes

and slept into the evenings when her legs would ache.

In a new journal, she wrote all of her names,

Hauwa Tini Adamu Geter, then nothing else.

When I shutter at the questions I cannot answer

in our birth country, my sister insists, *Mom*

would have been this way too.

It's cultural, she will say, needing

even cruel things to be simple—a laugh in her voice

I can't place. When my sister says, *Nigeria*,

her voice sounds starved to see our father again,

what with tickets so cheap, she suggests we return with him

to the country that can call his daughters' names

by blood, the land where our family will

ask why I haven't a husband.

Cousins, aunties sending theirs out

into the rainy season to fetch me one.

THE WAR ON TERROR

There was rain that December.
The same banners

for school dances. Soldiers came home
stating justification

over forgiveness.
Things got easier. Twice,

the story was, *yes*.
You can wait so long

for a word to come
it will fracture

at the hip. We welcomed soldiers
home and after could not say our names

in our own country.
In some future,

my nephews lob their belts
in the air, as if the sun

were a branch they could rest
their nooses upon.

They mistake the weight
of the body as necessary.

THE WIDOWER

Five winters in a row,

my father knuckles

the trunk of his backyard pine

like he's testing a watermelon.

He scolds smooth patches

where bark won't grow,

breaks branches

to find them hollow.

He inhales deeply

and the pine tree has lost

even its scent.

My father the backyard

forest king, the humble

king. The dragging his scepter

through the darkness king,

king who won't

lay his tenderness down

trembles into the black

unable to stop

his kingdom from dying.

THREE-HUNDRED GIRLS

1990

The heat in Nigeria doesn't care

that it's rainy season. That the mangos rot.

Of the sound of milk cans buckling in the pantry.

The lights have been gone, four days.

The houseboy returns

with gasoline, bread, warm bottles of orange soda.

It is an hour outside

evening. My sister waves

her passport like a fan.

Auntie Mairo and Auntie Asabe unwrap

their headscarves, their hair springing

like perennials. Inside each sigh they leave

a name, their bodies smelling

of a whole country.

2004

When Auntie Asabe picks us up from the airport,

she drives right up the landing strip.

Kano smells of ripened avocados and men

with semi-automatics. Laughing, she tells us the price

of petrol has been rising for weeks,

soon the whole country will strike.

At the compound, she waves to armed guards

keeping out thieves and militia.

We eat fufu, efo, and egusi soup.

My sister, bowl after bowl of jollof rice.

Like a woman no longer living

outside the language of her happiness,

my mother smiles with her teeth.

Her hands two bright shadows.

Auntie Mairo shakes her head and says their youngest brother

has disappeared plucking bees from his mind,

how their eldest comes to money.

The generator sputters in the distance.

No second wives

cloud their conversation.

2014

Switching between Hausa and English,

the ghost of my mother says, *A'aha!*

How do you steal three-hundred girls?

She begins listing names—Rejoice, Jummai,

Blessing. *Asabe, like your auntie,*
she says. *Hannatu like your Yaya.*

Fourteen Hauwas, like me,
she says, as though I've forgotten

mothers in Chibok are still
weeping on the floors of classrooms

burned into burial grounds.
My Nigerian passport

expires. The news calculates
their dowry at twelve

American dollars,
reports girls perish

of snakebites, malaria. The rest
by marriage.

HOW TO SAW A MAN IN HALF

Fascinated by the differences
in our grief, I yank gauze

out of my father's open heart
like a magician

pulling scarves,
until there is nothing,

only skin puckered back,
the gaping of his chest. Flooded

with saline, my father grimaces
from the teeth

of this intimacy:
My fingers pulling the hole in him

wide. The search for infection,
trap doors—his pulse,

trying to proffer a deal
between us to let him die.

With my hands in my father's chest
I will beg this loneliness to be the last.

Years later,
hip replacement two,

desperate for cover,
my father will find none,

only his daughter, halved
at the knees,

sopping his blood up
in fistfuls.

FELLING

After the maple came down

there was only rice

to eat, in my dreams,

my sister's son

playing with matches,

the way everything suddenly seemed

so expensive even the addicts on Albany got clean

and *can't you remember to shut the fucking cupboards*

fell through the ceiling

of my apartment every night,

I rode trains,

saw the circle the sun leaves in the water

between Boston and Connecticut.

I saw how I've always been

attracted to little

violences: my mother

making herself up

in the mirror,

my father heaving

into the barter

of his crown. The two

of them showing me

how to hide inside

a switchblade.

NAMING MY MOTHER

In hallways, in the kitchen:

Kai!

from your throat like spicy suya.

It meant *upset, astonished,*

your nerves *so tired.*

It was Africa happening

inside you. In other languages,

kai translates to *keeper of the keys,*

to *love*—

only Hausa

saturates the word

with phonemes, meaning *you* or

self, *carry*, or *reach*.

It means *to be equal to*,

to be enough—so much riding

on the intonation of a voice.

Mother, *Kai!*

taught me to listen.

To press my ear to the eye

of every stranger who butchered

your name, which, in our first language, still means

Adam's black Eve.

You wanted daughters instead of sons.

What you named your first-

born meant, *Beautiful.*

I was *Protector.*

So, when you kneeled East

in America, clean

for Isha'a, I wished you

a Nancy, a Beth.

Something so white

it appeared just washed.

Hauwa, all these years,

and still there is the murmur

of you. *Kai!*

a rattle in my throat,

our names two familiar

sounds turned strange,

tightropes swaying,

in a colonial country.

IDDAH

Only when the surgeon approaches
does my father stop crying.

His heart sputtering, spent.
The anesthesia a long-begged-for reprieve

from being a layman
in the mourning rooms

of women. Six weeks
my mother's been gone

and the surgeon drags
his fingers across my father's chest

explaining how three calf vessels
can rescue the heart.

Already gowned, my father listens
ambivalently, a thousand miles

from those first nights
where he lay side by side

with his grown daughter in his wife's bed.
The two of us desperate

to keep the other
breathing. In the morning,

he washed dishes, I dried.
Together, slowly domesticating

our suffering, both unsure
if his fatherhood could stand

up in the light.
From his hospital gurney,

my father gazes at me
as though staring across a fog-

covered lake. We are twins afraid
to be separated.

Years later, when I think of my father,
nurses wheeling him down that white corridor,

the growing distance between us
making his body

smaller, then smaller,

I will recognize

in us the rescuer's dilemma

and the drowning man

flailing out at sea.

My desire

to be the savior. Then, the choice:

Him or me.

HAJJ

All these years she's been gone? Allah still picks
                               her bones clean,
                               his mouth still drips
                               with her marrow.

How un-American. A stranger
                               on familiar land,
                               I touch my head East.
                               I say, *Allāhu* Akbar
                               my voice foreign
                               even unto him.

Who appears? The moon,
                               as though appearing
                               were a simple thing.

ACKNOWLEDGMENTS

With gratitude to the editors of the following publications, in which these poems first appeared.

92Y: "The Leaving"

Boston Review: "How to Bring Your Children to America"

Columbia Journal: "Naturalized Citizen"

Court Green: "Naming Ceremony," "The Widower"

Gulf Coast: "The War on Terror"

Linebreak: "Hymn"

Los Angeles Review of Books: "Visiting Prophets"

The Rumpus: "My Brother-In-Law Recites the Takbir"

Narrative Magazine: "The Life of a Cell," "Salah," "Felling"

The New Yorker: "The Break In"

Pinwheel Journal: "Family Portrait," "Eid al-Adha"

Tin House: "Testimony," "Testimony," "Testimony," "Testimony"

Two Peach: "How to saw a man in half," "Hajj"

West Branch: "Fajr," "Three-Hundred Girls"

With love and thanks to the friends, family, and teachers who have been my village, and with special thanks to the following for their support: my parents Tyrone and Hauwa Geter, Jamila Geter, Alieu Badjie, Nuh Badjie and Zayd Barkindo, Ryann Stevenson Brewer, Jeffrey Allen, Holly Amos, Abba Belgrave, Jay Deshpande, Joseph Mains, John Murillo, William Brewer, Stephen Danos, Kelly Forsythe, Brett Funderburk, Lizzie Harris, Darrel Alejandro Holnes, Stephanie Land, Ricardo Maldonado, Daniel Morgan, Catherine Pond, Ben Purkert, Andrey Radovski, Camille Rankine, Jess Rose, sam sax, Laura Seal, Ashley Toliver, the Cave Canem family, my teachers at Columbia College Chicago, and Suzanna Tamminen and the entire Wesleyan University Press team. And in memory, always, of Nathan Breitling and Catherine Simpson.

ABOUT THE AUTHOR

Born in Zaria, Nigeria, Hafizah Geter is a Nigerian-American writer and editor. She received a BA in English and economics from Clemson University and an MFA in poetry from Columbia College Chicago. Hafizah's poetry and prose have appeared in the *New Yorker*, *Tin House*, *Boston Review*, *Longreads*, and McSweeney's *Indelible in the Hippocampus*, among others. She lives in Brooklyn, New York.